IMAGES OF ENGLAND

Around Goole

IMAGES OF ENGLAND

Around Goole

Ben and Mave Chapman

NONSUCH

For Tommy,
Thomas Walter Armstrong (1904–1968),
a small return for all your love and encouragement throughout the years.
Mave.

First published 1997
This new pocket edition 2006
Images unchanged from first edition

Nonsuch Publishing Limited
The Mill, Brimscombe Port,
Stroud, Gloucestershire, GL5 2QG
www.nonsuch-publishing.com

Nosuch Publishing is an imprint of Tempus Publishing

ISBN 1-84588-275-x

Typesetting and origination by Nonsuch Publishing Limited
Printed in Great Britain by Oaklands Book Services Limited

Contents

Acknowledgements

When writing a reference book help comes from many different quarters.

We gratefully acknowledge the help of our niece Jane Conroy who cheerfully chauffeurs us around from place to place.

Goole Reference Library proved most helpful with research material; thanks to all the staff and particularly Colette Leetham.

A debt of gratitude is owed to Ann and Eric Hartley of Sheffield for their encouragement, loan of postcards and valuable historical information. Their great kindness has truly enhanced this book.

Thanks to our dear friend Wayne Wolton for his advice on taking the one or two modern photographs and also to Les Barker for the loan of material.

Special thanks to Arthur Credland of the Hull Town Docks Museum, and Hull City Museums and Art Galleries for the loan of the picture of the keel Ada by Reuben Chappell.

All reasonable attempts have been made to contact any copyright holders where applicable.

Ben and Mave Chapman
Withernsea 1997

Introduction

The history of Goole dates back hundreds of years. A map of 1362 shows the town of Goole marked as Gula, and in 1552 there is a record of a place called Golflete. By the seventeenth century this had become Goule, which is probably French in origin and means 'a hollow or creek in a deep river'.

The settlement at that time consisted of a few cottages by the river and is recorded as having been a fishing community. This is highly credible because in the 1930s a few local men still earned a little to supplement their meagre incomes by fishing for salmon and eels in the river. There was one road and a fine building known as Goole Hall, which was the home of the Empson family, who appear to have owned a considerable amount of land covering a large area later known as Goole Fields.

The farmland surrounding Goole, including many of the nearby villages, was produced by warping, which was, in a sense, a form of reclamation whereby fertile silt was deposited from the River Ouse, which was particularly rich and nutritious. It is possible that some of this silt was carried via the River Humber from the continuously eroding Holderness coastline. The region resembled the landscape of Holland, with its flat fields and innumerable rivers such as the Ouse, Wharfe, Derwent, Aire, Don and Trent.

In the seventeenth century, James I invited Cornelius Vermuyden (1595–1683), a Dutch engineer from Zeeland, who was considered the greatest contemporary expert on land drainage, to visit England to survey the area. Initially there were delays to the scheme and it was not until five years later, in 1626, that he signed an agreement with Charles I for what became the Dutch River Project.

The task was an enormous one, even for a man of his expertise. The marshy area which he was to drain was served by nine rivers: the Don, Idle, Torne, Aire, Bycarsdyke, Humber, Ouse, Trent and Went, all of which contributed to the state of the terrain by flooding when they were high. Vermuyden began by tackling the River Don which joined the River Aire at East Cowick. He made new cuts and junctions, incorporating the other rivers, but unfortunately he encountered further difficulties when the River Aire was unable to take all the extra water. Instead of achieving his task of draining the area, he had caused serious flooding, which understandably infuriated the local farmers – and he was prosecuted for his pains.

A solution was finally found by creating the Dutch River as a relief channel. It joined the River Ouse at Goole, which at that time was the place where vessels from the outlying villages of Airmyn, Howden, Saltmarshe, Whitton and Reedness waited for the tides. In spite of his difficulties, Vermuyden's reputation as an engineer grew; in 1629 he was knighted and, for a time, resided in Westminster. Another drainage scheme which further enhanced his reputation was the Fens and East Anglia Project.

Over the following decades Goole still remained a small, insignificant place. A census taken in 1821 shows a population of 450; the same census identifies Howden with 2,080, Thorne with 2,713 and Selby with 4,097 – all obviously thriving communities. This was soon to change. It is fair to say the Goole really owes its growth and prosperity to a gentleman called William Hammond Bartholomew.

Bartholomew was born at Lake Lock House, Stanley, on 13 January 1831. In 1851, at the age of 20, he continued a family tradition and joined the Aire and Calder Navigation Company in the engineering department. His father, who also worked for the firm, unfortunately died a year later. Within two years Bartholomew had proved his skills and, in 1853, he was made resident engineer. In that same year a gentleman called William Aldham, then aged 40, became the chairman of the company.

The two men devised a plan to counter competition from the railways and conceived an ambitious programme of canal building. The Aire and Calder Canal was one of their favoured projects and one of its special features was the type of traffic it was to carry. Bartholomew persuaded the board to sanction the building of three sets of compartment boats, each to carry 25 tons, and also to build hydraulic hoists at Goole to lift and discharge the tubs. The idea was patented in 1862 and began operation in 1865. The compartment boats were affectionately known in the area as 'Tom Puddings'; each had buffers and they were linked together like railway wagons. A wire rope at each side allowed the bargemen in charge of the towing vessel to steer them. These 'trains' varied between ten and thirty 'Tom Puddings' and made it possible for coal from the collieries of the West Riding of Yorkshire to be transported in large volumes at a very cheap and competitive rate. On reaching their destination at Goole, each compartment was lifted by one of the special hoists, known locally as the 'Pepperpot Hoists' because of their upper structure, in a contraption rather like a cage, and tipped directly into the hold of a sea going vessel.

During this period Bartholomew spent a considerable amount of his time in Goole and had his own suite of rooms at the Lowther Hotel. In contrast, the navvies who actually built the canal were housed in huts which had been specially provided near the same hotel. Needless to say, they were hard working, hard living men whose activities during their meagre leisure hours were often more than lively!

The Act of Parliament which enabled the Aire and Calder Navigation Company to build the canal from Knottingley to Goole also provided for two small docks to be constructed. These were known as Ship Dock and Barge Dock, and were opened in 1826, a date which has since been considered as the time when Goole as a town became a reality. The earliest terraces were built in the 1830s and the town progressed from there.

At 11.00 am on 26 July 1826, apparently after a few days delay caused by drought, the canal was officially opened. Spectators gathered at Ferry Bridge to witness the departure of a procession consisting of four fly boats, followed by over forty vessels. Between 3.00 pm and 4.00 pm they reached Barge Dock in Goole, where they were greeted by a large crowd. A dinner party was held at the Banks Arms and at around 8.00 pm that evening, the steam packet Lowther arrived, decked out in the colours of various nations. The entire workforce who had been employed on the project in the town were given free refreshments.

In 1883 Bartholomew successfully opposed an attempt to build a bridge across the River Humber. This added to the gratitude in which he was held by the people of Goole who already lauded him not only for the employment and prosperity he had brought to the town, but also for his philanthropic gestures, which included the provision of a church and a hospital. However, grief stricken by the death of his wife in 1916, the famous engineer's health rapidly deteriorated to the point that the Aire and Calder Board decided to relieve him of his duties, and granted him an annuity of £500. Sadly he was not to enjoy this for very long; he died on 9 November 1919 at the age of 88.

The system of transportation that he had introduced on the Aire and Calder Canalcontinued to be used; it may be said to have reached its apogee just prior to the First World War, when an amazing 500,000 tons were carried. After a slow start the port began to prosper as other services were provided. A 50 hp paddle driven tug was available to tow sailing vessels along the Rivers Ouse and Humber to the point from which they could sail when the tide was right, and ships were also brought into Goole by this means. In what could be loosely described as a tourist venture, passengers were taken along the canal from the town by a catamaran drawn by four, or sometimes six horses ridden by boys dressed as jockeys.

Apart from coal, Goole was now handling cargoes of logwood from South America and trading with European ports. There are stories of how, in the 1870s, a cargo of 120 tons of dynamite docked at the port, much to the consternation of the residents. As Goole moved into the twentieth century trade was booming and its population had rapidly increased. By 1911, the census registered a population of 20,916.

Unfortunately the First World War greatly affected the port's trade, not least because of the enemy occupation of many of the places with which it had previously conducted business. Between the two World Wars, whilst its coal exports remained reasonably high, its import trade did not fare so well and the improvements which were made to the port with the opening of Ocean Lock in 1938 did not have an opportunity to prove beneficial because of the declaration of war once more in 1939.

Geographically the town has always occupied a somewhat awkward position as a result of a river which, at certain times, was difficult to navigate. It was beset over the years by attempts by the Port of Hull to blight its trade and from competition, to varying degrees, from numerous small wharves on the River Ouse and River Trent, such as Howdendyke. The town has struggled valiantly to maintain the status it once had as a place of importance with its canal and river traffic, but it is constantly facing the demands of new technology and ideas.

Goole can also claim one other citizen who has done much to enhance its reputation and, perhaps, unwittingly leave an invaluable record of its history. The artist Reuben Chappell was born in the town on 21 July 1870, the youngest of six children. At the time of his birth his father was a joiner who later became a master cabinet maker.

Reuben was raised near the docks and from early childhood was familiar with ships and seafarers; from late infancy he demonstrated a talent for drawing ships. He won a scholarship to the privately owned Grammar School for boys, became interested in photography and was apprenticed to a local photographer. It is thought that tinting photographic prints led him into painting. In his late teens he was producing line drawings for a local newspaper and began to earn for himself a reputation for painting ships. At about this time he established a studio at No.7 Jackson Street. He advertised his services as a photographer and painter, but had little time for his camera as his paintings were eagerly sought by seamen. He was a familiar figure at the docks as the ships arrived, sketching and taking commissions. His charge for a water colour was 5s (25p) and 30s (£1.50) for an oil painting.

He was very prolific, producing in the region of 12,000 paintings in his lifetime but sadly, not many have survived. He was very modest about his art and never had an exhibition or showed in galleries, although today his work commands high prices. Married at twenty-five he was content as a professional artist to provide for his family but was forced eventually, due to bronchial trouble, to leave the town and move to Cornwall.

Reuben Chappell paintings not only rank highly for their merit and bring kudos to the town of Goole, but also provide a marvellous record of the ships, both sail and steam, that frequented the port at the time. They make an invaluable contribution to the town's history. Chappell died in 1940 and his work is displayed in his native town – of which he would not doubt have approved.

Since the boundary changes this century, Goole is no longer in the West Riding of Yorkshire but has become part of the new county of East Yorkshire. Today, the chief interest for tourists still lies in the docks and the canal but for the curious visitor and resident alike, the excellent facilities of the town's library and museum bear testament to Goole's history and community.

One

Goole the Town

Here we have a glimpse of the town centre of Goole with different aspects of Boothferry Road, including a busy market day and the railway station early in the twentieth century.

When the docks were opened in 1836, Goole had 450 inhabitants. The earliest buildings, which were terraces of plain, three storey brick houses were erected in Aire Street. They are thought to date from 1830 and have been described as some of the most interesting in the town. The railway, seen to the left of the picture, was not part of the main line but more of a shunting area for the docks traffic. Businesses were soon established. Some of these family concerns served the town for many years and became household names there; one such was James Hopley & Sons, who sold fruit and vegetables and also had a stall in the market.

This view of Aire Street shows a shunting engine conveying a wagon which appears to be loaded with barrels. On the right is a shop on the corner offering wines and spirits for sale, with two small boys playing with a whip and top, oblivious to the photographer – unlike the men in the centre who pose accordingly. All are sporting the standard headgear of a black flat cap, with a variety of jackets and coats. A little further down the street are the Globe Dining Rooms.

A busy scene near the junction of Boothferry Road and Stanhope Street, clearly showing the Bank Chambers and St John's Buildings, with a crane and ship's mast in the distant dock. The horse-drawn vehicle in the centre appears to be heading towards Boothferry Road and is a working vehicle; the other, to the right, is of a much lighter construction.

Boothferry Road during the Edwardian period. There is a Blackburn's tailors and a Freeman Hardy & Willis shoe shop, both of which traded for some decades in the town. To the left, the building which advertises umbrellas and mantles on its upper windows bears the name 'W. Royston' on its fascia board. The traffic is strictly one horse power, including what appears to be a very large load being driven down the middle of the road!

Above: Church Street, or St Johns Street, as it was sometimes known, in 1925. To the right are the railway lines used for the local movement of goods; to the left, the Goole Steam Shipping offices. The building with the white frontage is the bank and the shop in the centre is that of Jackson & Dixon, high class grocers.

Left: Jackson & Dixon were grocers covering all aspects of the trade: wholesale, retail and, very importantly, supplying shipping. Every inch of the shop front is used in some way to promote their products in this Edwardian photograph. Perhaps the most intriguing is the offer of their own special brand of tea, which they describe as the 'finest the world produces at the price': 1s 7d (8p) per lb. Mild cured ham, cheese and dates are also featured, as well as the poultry hung above the entrance.

arket Day, Goole.

The cast-iron framed Victorian indoor market was built to replace an earlier market which was destroyed by fire. The new market hall was officially opened on 22 October 1896. In 1981–82 another hall was built alongside to extend the facility. This busy scene shows outside traders in the late 1920s. To the left is the fruit and vegetable stall of James Hopley & Sons, who also had a shop in Aire Street. To the right is Anthony White's stall 'For pure elite Ices'. The mother of that family, Antonia Bianca, had an ice cream shop in Chapel Street. The family was, of course, Italian. Their daughter, Mary, was fondly known as 'Ice Cream Mary'; they changed their name to White in the 1930s. Anthony, or Antonio, as most local people called him, would travel the streets of the town with a beautifully painted cart selling his delicious ice cream. Some high spirited children would dance around him singing the old music hall song Oh, Oh, Antonio, which he apparently enjoyed and accepted in a good natured manner. The notice board above Hopley's stall bears the letters 'GUDC' – Goole Urban District Council.

The Cinema Picture House could seat 1,000 people and was very proud of its patent tip up seats and electric lights. This postcard, sent in 1921, shows the original front elevation which was 'modernised' in the early 1930s. The shop on the right was the Dainty Sweet Stores and, on the left is Harry Boom's tailors shop. After the large fronted building can be seen Bickerton & Sons and the Goole Times, the printers who produced the local newspaper, town guide books and other such material. Next is the Lyceum Cafe and then de Cobain's bicycle shop, with Marriot's bootmakers shop next door. The scene is very different today with a supermarket and modern shops.

A later view of the Cinema Palace on Boothferry Road, with posters advertising current and forthcoming films. Instead of a horse and cart we now have a motor car progressing along the street.

A. F. de Cobain,

Boothferry Road, Goole.

"RALEIGH."

Note these Names! Note these Prices!

		£	s.	d.
RALEIGH CYCLES from		5	5	0
☞ ,, ,, Three Speed ...		9	15	0
HUMBER CYCLES from		7	7	0
SINGER from		7	10	0
☞ SUNBEAM (with little Oil Bath) from ...		14	14	0
ELSWICK from		8	8	0
☞ PREMIER from		8	8	0
ALBERT from		4	4	0

Value and Quality Seldom if ever Equalled. Never Beaten.

Large Stock of all Accessories. Repairs efficiently Executed.

Official Repairer to the C.T.C.

Tyres and Tyre Repairs a Speciality.

Vulcanising done on the Premises.

Plating and enamelling of very best style and finish.

Free Wheels and Change Speed Gears Fitted.

A. F. de COBAIN,

——— BOOTHFERRY ROAD, GOOLE.

This advertisement from around 1933 is from a well-known cycle business. The de Cobain family had premises in Goole for many years, the business being handed down from father to son. In the 1930s cycling was very popular. Not only was it a convenient way to travel to and from work, especially for those previously obliged to walk, but it also became a popular leisure pursuit. Note the amazing prices; a bicycle could be purchased for as little as £5.00. In later years, to move with the times, the family sold radios and later, televisions.

Goole. — Boothferry Road, East.

Boothferry Road East. Outside Clarkson's, to the left, are two excellent examples of one of the favourite modes of transport in the early part of the twentieth century. The bicycle was widely used by people of all social levels for work and pleasure. The window of the *Goole Times* displays some of the many things which they produced, including postcards. The shop next door, on the corner, shows the ornate name sign of Bickerton & Son.

Here the Goole Times Co. Ltd advertise their services to the district and parish councils. They are promoting their works in the hope of attracting business which, along with producing the local newspaper, catered for many aspects of the printing trade.

The clock which stands opposite the market where the road branches to North Street on the left and Carlisle Street on the right. The clock tower itself bears the dates 1826 and 1926. Originally, as seen here, there were public lavatories beneath it but now it stands rather incongruously on a grassy traffic mound. The men leaning against the railed wall are typical of the scene; it seemed to attract elderly and at some periods, unemployed men, who simply watched the world go by or gathered to exchange views. On the right side of the road near the market, the Cinema Picture House is now no longer there; in its place is a supermarket and the whole character of Boothferry Road has changed.

The railway crossed Boothferry Road on its way to Doncaster and the West Riding. Pedestrians could use the subways on each side of the road, on the left and right of the picture. Many older people remember, with fond amusement, the elderly gentleman who spent his days singing hopefully for pennies under the subway on the Pasture Road side. He had but one song, an old music hall number entitled My Grandfather's Clock. When a train was due the signalman in his box on the right would swing the gates across to stop any traffic in the road. This view was taken around 1920, possibly a little earlier. There are signs on the road of the passing of horses and the occasional cyclist but no motor vehicles.

Pasture Road, which runs along behind the railway station to the right as one travels along Boothferry Road from east to west. The right side is obviously mainly residential but there were some shops further down; the left had a variety of interesting goods on offer. There was Bateman's, selling primarily sweets and tobacco but which also ran a 2d (4p) lending library, managed by a very gentlemanly proprietor. The larger shop just past the parked van is that of Edmond Gibbins' dress shop; to own an outfit from Gibbins was socially desirable and the fortunate lady would be the envy of her friends.

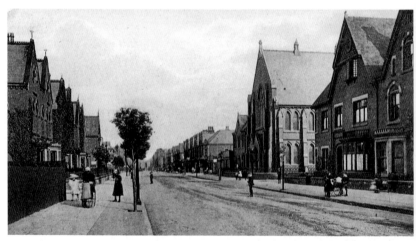

Boothferry Road from the west end, looking down towards the town. The usual Victorian houses and chapel are evident and it is interesting to see ladies pausing for a few minutes gossip whilst giving baby an airing. Close examination of the scene further down the road reveals busy activity in the shops.

William Hammond Bartholomew, who was responsible for the development of the town, was known to his business associates as a hard man, but there was another side to him which was very caring, especially for those less fortunate than himself. Many of his philanthropic gestures were anonymous and therefore never recognised, but he gave £11,000 to provide a hospital for the town. The Bartholomew Cottage Hospital was to care for Goole's sick for many years.

The Secondary School, or Goole Grammar School as it became known in 1933, for boys and girls was opened in September 1909, the foundation stone being laid by Mr Thomas Coates Turton on 23 July 1908. The first headmaster there was Mr C.J. Forth MA, BSc. In 1929, around the time of this view, the buildings were extended to accommodate 500 pupils. In 1933 the charter which raised the town to Borough status was presented in the school grounds by Prince George KG to the Charter Mayor, Councillor T.E. Kettlewell, who was also a governor of the school. The school motto was Alte Pete – aim high. The Memorial Gardens, evident in the foreground, were laid out in 1922, the site being given by the Aire and Calder Navigation. The cenotaph is a copy on a smaller scale of that in Whitehall, London. Both gardens and cenotaph were provided predominantly by public subscription.

Parish Church, Goole

24/ 4/ 05.

CHANCEL, PARISH CHURCH, GOOLE.

40485

Right: Not surprisingly, St John's was approached from Church Street. This view gives an excellent profile of the fine spire supported by flying buttresses. It can be seen from the river for many miles and from some of the villages, such as Swinefleet.

Below: St Joseph's Roman Catholic Church, the tower of which can be seen at the end of Pasture Road. The church also had a hall which was used for many social functions, not only by members of the church, but also by citizens of the town, many of whom have happy memories of dances and parties which were organised by various respectable societies such as the Sons of Temperance.

105.51. THE PARISH CHURCH
GOOLE.

Opposite above: This fine view of the parish church of St John shows its close proximity to the docks. It was built by the Aire and Calder Navigation between 1843–48. It is a very large, impressive building and the architects were William Hurst and W.R. Moffat. The style is based on the Perpendicular, as can be seen by the stately windows.

Opposite below: St John's church chancel, altar and pulpit in 1908. Inside the church there are some unusual commemorative items dedicated to heroes of land and sea. There is an inscription dedicated to a citizen who ran to his death leading his men in 1914 in the First World War and another window shows a man with an aeroplane over his head. The men of Colne, who sailed from Goole and whose ship sank in the North Sea in 1906 with the loss of twelve lives are honoured, as are those who died in 1931 when the Calder sank.

Left: The old coat of arms of Goole town. The steam and sail powered ship represents the importance of the port, whilst the white rose signifies Yorkshire.

Below: This official coat of arms was granted to Goole Borough Council on 7 October 1933. The blazon reads: 'Arms: Or a lymphad sails set and oars in action sable, flags flying to the dexter gules, on a chief of the second three swans argent. Supporters: On either side a Viking supporting in the dexter hand a spear proper.' The Viking refers to the North Sea raiders who settled in the area whilst the lymphad, or galley, refers to the seafaring and commerce of the town. The swans are from the arms of Selby Abbey, once a considerable land owner in the area.

One of the most prominent structures in Goole is the water tower. The first one was built around 1883 and the second, pictured opposite, was built in 1926 to provide for the needs of a growing town.

This comparison between the two water towers clearly highlights the difference in size of the older, narrower, red brick version and the much later concrete tower with its more realistic capacity for the twentieth century.

Old Goole is a continuation of the town on the other side of the river. After the railway station is Mariners Street which leads to the bridges crossing the docks and finally to the Dutch River Bridge. On the left at this point is the road into Old Goole which eventually leads to Swinefleet, Whitgift and the Reedness area. Old Goole was the home of Cragg's Shipyard where many fine ships were constructed over the years. On the left of the photograph are a garage and petrol pump and the large building to the right is obviously a tobacconists.

Here we have just turned the corner leading from the town down Victoria Street. The large building on the left is the Victoria Hotel, always a popular hostelry. To the right is the river bank leading to Riverside Gardens.

The junction of Marshfield Road and Hook Road, with the beginning of Riverside Gardens on the right. The First World War tank was a popular plaything for local youngsters and was treated as a modern child would use a climbing frame. It is hard to imagine that this was the original intention for the tank when it was first placed here; a far more likely reason would be as a grim reminder of the men who left their home town, never to return. It was removed in the early days of the Second World War along with the park railings to provide metal for the war effort.

Hook Road in 1905, long before Riverside Gardens was laid out. The town and church spire can be seen in the distance and on the left is a pedestrian path along the river bank, with just a glimpse of the river. The stately looking houses to the right, between Salisbury Avenue and Fountain Street, were mostly converted into flats in the 1950s and 1960s.

A view of Goole from the river bank near Riverside Gardens at the bowling green end. The small boats were used by local fishermen who, in season, caught salmon and eels.

The path along the bank of the River Ouse as it flows from Goole towards the village of Hook. The family are obviously enjoying the occasion. Is it perhaps the father's little fishing boat they are watching, or has he just come ashore to show his catch to the older members of the party? The Saltmarshe bank of the river is evident on the right.

Riverside Gardens was the first public park to be laid out in Goole. It was conceived at the beginning of the First World War and covered over 3 acres. The bandstand was a popular feature; a number of folding chairs are already in place for a concert in this view from the early 1930s.

A more general view of Riverside Gardens which was situated between Hook Road and the river bank. There was a pavilion, a shelter and public lavatories in the park. The bowling green was near the trees in the centre of this photograph and there was also one tennis court which was very well patronised.

In 1874 the first Goole Burial's Board was elected to discuss whether the cemetery should cover 4 or 8 acres; a majority vote advocated the 8 acre plan. The chapels and curator's house were erected in 1877 and part of the area consecrated. The cemetery provided burial space for the Parish of Goole and, when it became the urban district, for the whole area. In 1907 a further 5 ½ acres was added and in 1933, another 10 acres which at the time was hoped to meet the needs of the district for many years. It is a well appointed, tranquil amenity with mature trees and a variety of shrubs along the walkways. For many years children and their fathers spent numerous happy hours searching around the horse chestnut trees for 'conkers' during the autumn months.

Left: Goole, like other Yorkshire towns such as Hull, did not escape the Zeppelin raids during the First World War. In Goole Cemetery there is a monument dedicated to the sixteen people who died during one such raid; they range from an 8 month baby to 74 year old lady. The inscription reads: 'In Memorium. In memory of sixteen citizens of Goole who lost their lives by A German Zeppelin Raid on 9th August 1915. "Eternal Rest give unto them O Lord."'

Opposite above: The names listed on the marble book are: Left side, Sarah Acaster, aged 65 years; Sarah Ann Acaster, aged 34 years; Kezia Acaster, aged 38 years; Violet Stainton, aged 18 years; Hannah Goodall, aged 74 years. Right side: Florence Harrison, aged 4 years; Alice Harrison, aged 6 years; Margaret Selina Pratt, aged 8 months; Agnes Pratt, aged 30 years; Grace Woodhall, aged 31 years; Mary Carroll, aged 32 years; James Carroll, aged 36 years; Alice Carroll, aged 4 years; Gladys Mary Carroll, aged 3 years; Alice Smith, aged 17 years.

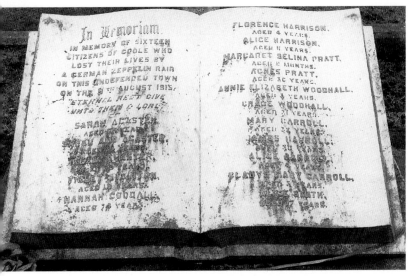

In **Memoriam**.
IN MEMORY OF SIXTEEN
CITIZENS OF GOOLE WHO
LOST THEIR LIVES BY
A GERMAN ZEPPELIN RAID
ON THIS UNDEFENDED TOWN
ON THE 9 TH AUGUST 1915.
ETERNAL REST GIVE
UNTO THEM O LORD.

SARAH ACASTER
AGED 51 YEARS
EMILY ANN ACASTER
AGED 28 YEARS
ROLLO ACASTER
AGED 6 YEARS
VIOLET STANTON
AGED 13 YEARS
HANNAH GOODALL
AGED 79 YEARS

FLORENCE HARRISON.
AGED 4 YEARS.
ALICE HARRISON.
AGED 6 YEARS.
MARGARET SELINA PRATT.
AGED 11 MONTHS.
AGNES PRATT.
AGED 30 YEARS.
ANNIE ELIZABETH WOODHALL.
AGED 3 YEARS.
GRACE WOODHALL.
AGED 31 YEARS.
MARY CARROLL.
AGED 33 YEARS.
JAMES CARROLL.
AGED 10 YEARS.
ALICE CARROLL.
AGED 8 YEARS.
GLADYS MARY CARROLL.
AGED 3 YEARS.
ALICE SMITH.
AGED 47 YEARS.

Below: West Park, the largest park in the town was laid out in 1932 in Airmyn Road, and covered 32 acres. The Unemployment Grants Committee contributed towards the cost of approximately £15,500. A popular amenity was the bandstand where regular weekend concerts were held; there were also shelters, tea rooms and public lavatories. For the more energetic there was a bowling green and tennis courts, both grass and hard, which was the venue for local tournaments in the summmer months. There was also a paddling pool, a model yacht pond and a children's playground. An oak tree was planted by Prince George when he visited for the Charter in 1933.

The village of Airmyn is built on the banks of the River Aire as it flows to merge with the River Ouse at Boothferry. A river bank was built, probably early in the development of the village, to contain the water at high tide and to minimise the danger of flooding. The long, winding High Street followed the curves of the river. This view, from the turn of the century, shows some of the brick cottages with their pantiled roofs. Since 1865 the village has been dominated by a clock tower, designed by J.J. Lockwood and paid for by the villagers in memory of George Percy, Lord of the Manor and Earl of Beverley who became Duke of Northumberland in 1865.

The river has always been important to Airmyn; not only did it provide reeds and warp for building but boats plied regularly providing transport. From medieval times until the eighteenth century it was customary for the deceased to be taken by boat for burial at Snaith. This was a much simpler and shorter way than taking to the roads with a horse drawn conveyance.

Airmyn Ferry, Goole.

Airmyn Ferry provided a link with the hamlet of Little Airmyn on the opposite bank of the river. Without this amenity, a journey of approximately 17 miles round by Snaith and Drax was involved which, apart from other considerations, was very time consuming.

Boothferry before the road bridge was constructed in 1929. The ferry was operated by Robert Lightfowler of the Percy Arms, who was helped by his sons. For light loads and few people, a rowing boat was used, but there was also a motor driven ferry which could carry small vehicles ranging from a pony and trap to a family car and occasionally, a hearse. The energetic way to attract the ferryman when standing on the Goole side was to simply shout and wave a handkerchief.

10515 BOOTHFERRY BRIDGE

ARJAY SERIES

Boothferry Bridge was built in 1929 by the Cleveland Bridge and Engineering Company. The structure is multi-span, the centre section being moveable to allow river access down the River Ouse to the town of Selby. There were those who saw the bridge as a remarkable feat of engineering while most of the local population thought it 'a bit of a novelty'. In fact it provided a vital link between the West Riding and the city of Kingston upon Hull. By 1970 it was estimated to be carrying about 30,000 vehicles a day on a two lane highway. In 1975 the Ouse Bridge Flyover linked Goole with the M62, about half a mile from the bridge, which is said to have taken its name from the original ferry crossing. Boothferry Bridge is now used mainly by cyclists and pedestrians and fortunately it has not been deemed necessary to remove this familiar landmark.

Two

People and Events

Children from St Joseph's who danced round the maypole at the Catholic Gymkhana in 1913. There are eight little couples, but what is surprising is that whilst the girls are all fairly similarly dressed, the boys range from one young man in shirt sleeves and one with no white collar to some in a variety of collars form a neat Eton type to the quite elaborate reaching right across the shoulders. Note the splendid bows in the girls' hair.

Left: An artist's impression of the Dutch engineer Cornelius Vermuyden (1595–1683) taken from an early print.

Below: The Dutch River around the turn of the twentieth century. On the right is Vermuyden Terrace and to the left, the shipyard. In the centre is the bridge which joins Goole to Old Goole; beyond the span of the bridge lies the Aire and Calder Canal. The foreground shows the mouth of the river as it runs into the River Ouse.

Opposite above: A large crowd has gathered outside the Ferryboat Inn on Vermuyden Terrace to watch the launch of a ship from Goole Shipbuilding Yard. The scene is very different today as much has been demolished.

Opposite below: Typical of the nautical paintings of Reuben Chappell is his depiction of the Hull keel Ada, captained by J. Gardner and painted in about 1890.

LAUNCH IN DUTCH RIVER. G[T.]

The Goole Regatta was recorded in July 1906 by local photographer Harrison of Sydney Street, Goole. Here we see the serious contenders.

Above: The Tub Race: an event in the 1906 Goole Regatta which appears to have some very enthusiastic entrants who are giving it their all!

Opposite: Thomas Walter Armstrong, known to all and sundry as Tommy, wearing the chain of office of Grand Worthy Patriarch of the Hull Grand Division of the Sons of Temperance in the 1930s. Born at Rawcliffe, he spent most of his adult life in the village of Hook and in Goole. After leaving school he worked at Rawcliffe Bridge paper mill, then as a surface man at Thorne Colliery. He went to Thorne for a bigger wage when his daughter was born and cycled from Hook to work every day. Tommy finally secured a job, for which he was long remembered, working on the Aire and Calder Navigation and moved to Goole. He was a jovial character and very popular with the people along the canal that he met in the course of his work.

Above: A section of the 1st Goole Troop Boy Scouts in 1910 at camp in Hornsea, East Yorkshire. The message on the back of this postcard tells that the photograph was taken just after the boys had been on a march. The other members had apparently been employed in camp duties. The writer also tells how he recently drilled a troop of Girl Guides and unwittingly informed them that he would 'soon make men of them'!

Right: The Boy Scout movement was very popular in the 1920s after the First World War. This Goole Scout wears the traditional hat, lanyards and badges. Taken in May 1921, the photograph was sent to 'Dear Father and Mother'.

Opposite: This diminutive fellow posing in the studio of Brigg's Photographers, Boothferry Road, Goole, around 1910, is wearing a General Post Office uniform.

A. HEPWORTH, age 5, 16 Miles, Time 1hr. 40m.

Left: The back of this postcard bears the inscription: Cycle Agent, Alfred Hepworth, Gowthorpe Street, Selby. The young lad is A. Hepworth (was this Alfred as a lad?) who cycled 16 miles in 1 hr 40 mins – quite an achievement for a five-year-old.

Below: Thomas Armstrong was a farm labourer at Potter's Grange Farm near Goole. Around the turn of the century he met and married a local girl, Bella Steels, a cook at Rawcliffe Hall. On a foggy November evening, within five years of their marriage, he was returning to their small cottage after work. To do so he had to cross the railway line near Goole Engine Sheds where he was fatally injured by a railway engine, leaving Bella to bring up their two sons, Thomas and Cliff. This was possibly one of the earliest railway fatalities in the area.

Opposite: Bella Parrot with her two sons Tom and Cliff in the garden of her home at No.19 Bell Lane, Rawcliffe, around 1920. The old mangle was kept near the wall during the summer and used by Bella and her neighbour Ciss. At the bottom of the garden was a shared wash house with a copper, the fire of which needed to be lit very early each morning to provide hot water. The copper had to be filled beforehand with buckets of water which had to be carried there from the pump by the house; the mangle was stored there during the cold winter months. The houses also shared a 'privy', with adjacent adult and child sized holes in the wooden plank seat, and a midden for the rubbish which could not be burned.

In 1913, when this picture was taken, Goole was a prosperous and thriving community. Here we see a float which was part of the Whit Walk, preparing to leave from the church. The horse waits patiently; it was accepted practice that traders would loan their horses and carts for this annual event, often being proud to be of service to their church or chapel.

The 1913 Whit Walk procession. The float is very elaborate and many hours have obviously been devoted to its construction. The procession usually passed Boothferry Road and, in later years, it proceeded to Hook Road. Hymns were sung and a service was held near Riverside Park. On this occasion the streets were crowded with spectators so perhaps a little was collected by way of donations for the local Sunday Schools.

The Primitive Methodist Church Guild float, 1919. The date, Union Jacks, soldier and nurse may suggest that it was a tribute to those who served in the First World War.

Another Primitive Methodist Church Guild float in 1919, representing Victory. Some of the participants are dressed in European costume, with a nurse and Boy Scout. The figure of Britannia symbolises the recent victory in the First World War.

This float, relating a story from the Bible, has been erected on the back of a lorry as opposed to the earlier horse and cart.

A family group depicted on a postcard sent as a Christmas greeting, bearing the message 'With love from us all at Escourt Street, Goole. Merry Christmas.' A further message pencilled in at the side says, 'Hope you like this' and it is signed 'Annie'. There is no indication as to the recipient or the date, and who was Annie – the lady standing, or seated? The clothes suggest that it is the 1930s, particularly the boy's jersey and tie. This is a poignant reminder of a street that no longer exists.

Three

Docks

Goole stands in the flat countryside at the confluence of the River Ouse and the River Don, which is known as the Dutch River until it reaches Snaith. This composite view emphasises the importance of shipping and docks to the town with just a glimpse of Boothferry Road, the main thoroughfare and the road out of town to the village of Hook.

This permit must not be allowed out of the possession of the Holder, and every precaution should be taken to prevent loss. Lost permits will only be renewed after strict investigation, which might entail delay.

189—1940

GOOLE DOCKS —
PROTECTED PLACES

PERMIT TO ENTER.

No. 188   Date of Issue   3rd April 1940

PORT OF GOOLE EMERGENCY COMMITTEE.

GOOLE DOCKS — PROTECTED PLACES.

PERMIT TO ENTER.

Signature of Chairman :

H.R. Ebbery.

Signature of Employer :

C Macland

Signature and Address of Holder :

J W Armstrong
11 Frederick St.,
Goole, Yks.

Nature of Employment :

Port Authority Staff.

Reg'd No. (Dockers) or
National Regn. No.   *KMYT 190/1*

Purpose for which Issued :

General Duties

The Holder of this Permit ... from entering any ... places :

No. 5 Swing Bridge

Goole Repair Yard

Hydraulic Power Station

Entrance Locks

Victoria Pier

Lowther Bridge

A. & C.N. Coaling Appliances

L.M.S. Coaling Appliances

Ships of Neutral Foreign Countries

Railways on the Dock Estate are subject to the Regulations of the L.M.S. Railway Co.

Tommy directing operations on his dredger on the Aire and Calder Canal. His knowledge of his craft and particular conditions pertaining to the canal came from years of experience. He was particularly pleased when engineers commissioned to build a new dredger asked him if he would be prepared to share his knowledge and make constructive suggestions about the design of the proposed new vessel.

Opposite: Wartime Goole Docks Permit issued to Tommy Armstrong in 1940, giving him access to the docks during a time of high security. Tommy worked for the Aire and Calder Navigation for some years as a mud boat man, unloading river mud by filling wheelbarrows and trundling the loads ashore by means of wooden planks between boat and bank. The mud boats were themselves filled by large dredgers. It was considered work of national importance keeping the docks dredged and in good working order and, as such, was declared a reserved occupation. This did not suit Tommy at all. He yearned to join the Navy in submarine service and volunteered twice, being rejected both times because of his work. Like many others he contented himself with ARP duties for the war effort. He eventually became a dredging foreman working the Leeds–Pontefract area of the Aire and Calder Canal. Sadly he died two months before he was due to retire in 1968.

Ship Dock and the canal were both built in 1826; Aldham Dock, named after William Aldham, was opened in 1882. When Bartholomew planned his canal scheme, Aldham was the Chairman of the Aire and Calder Navigation. The two men collaborated to advantage, Bartholomew providing the engineering skills. Together they produced an ambitious scheme which was to prove highly successful.

Ouse Dock was built in 1880. This early photograph shows fine sailing ships, barges and also two examples of the famous 'Pepperpot Hoists'.

An excellent panoramic view of the lock gates with ships entering on the tide. Several rafts of 'Tom Puddings' containing coal to be unloaded onto the ships can be seen at the bottom right.

The Basin was also completed in 1880. Another early view shows sailing ships and some of the famous 'Tom Puddings', or compartment boats, filled with coal.

An early photograph of Railway Dock around 1904, showing a variety of vessels from stately sailing ships to small steam coasters. As the name implies, Railway Dock's prime purpose was to deal with cargoes transported by rail either for export, or imported goods to be delivered elsewhere by the rail network.

Advertisement for the services offered by the Aire and Calder Navigation which appeared in the *Goole Times Illustrated Almanack*, 1933. It was the foresight of Bartholomew and the company who built the canal between Knottingly and Goole that was responsible for changing Goole from an obscure fishing village into an important port.

An excellent view of Lowther Bridge, behind which a ship is moored. Towering in the centre is the 'Pepperpot Hoist', so named because of its upper structure. The man seated to the left is obviously on some kind of duty; it has been suggested, in view of his flag, that he was concerned with the swinging of the bridge.

Cragg's Shipyard viewed from Ocean Lock. The yard was situated in Old Goole and reached by road over the bridges. Whenever a ship was to be launched people congregated on the Ocean Lock side to watch the event.

Coal was carried from the Yorkshire pits down the Aire and Calder Canal for over 120 years to Goole from where it was shipped to the Continent via the North Sea. By 1914 there were five hydraulically operated 'Pepperpot Hoists' which tipped the coal into the holds of waiting vessels. It has been said that this was one of the most effective systems to be used on waterways anywhere in the world. The last cargo was dealt with in 1986 by the No.5 hoist. The last two surviving hoists, No.3 on Aldham Dock and No.5 on South Dock, were listed for preservation but No.3 was badly damaged and had to be demolished. However No.5 is now intended as an exhibit for visitors to the Goole Docks complex.

A 'Pepperpot Hoist' clearly showing the cradle used to lift and discharge the coal from 'Tom Puddings', which carried 25 tons of coal. Bartholomew patented his idea in 1862; it became a reality when it began working in 1865.

The Promenade early in the twetnieth century. At high tide there were always people watching the ships arrive and depart: a popular pastime, especially in summer. Visitors were often taken there by their hosts to enjoy what, for a city dweller, was a real novelty. Here the lock gates have been opened. In the centre a group of ships are waiting to enter the port, lined up on the Hook Road bank of the River Ouse.

Lock Hill, a popular venue at tide time when people gathered to watch the movements of the ships. This early view from around 1900 shows a three-masted sailing ship in the centre, the lock gates and, to the right, the bollards used for mooring ships in dock.

The docks with a variety of vessels including a large coaster; the church dominates the scene. To the left is a large crane as opposed to the 'Pepperpot Hoists' which were used solely for unloading coal.

It was with high hopes of attracting more trade to the docks that Ocean Lock was built in the 1930s. It was opened in 1938 but before its real potential could be realised, the Seond World War began in 1939. Here its situation in relation to the coal hoist and some of the other docks is clear. The ship in the foreground, the Munster, was a regular visitor.

A diverse selection of traffic in Ocean Lock. On the right is the Munster and on the left, the Robrix, one of the famous Rix boats, each of which was designated with the suffix 'rix' on the end of its name. Father and daughter are clearly enjoying watching the ships in the lock.

One of the famous Abbey boats, the *Fountains Abbey* in Ocean Lock – proof that the dock could accommodate large vessels, as is borne out by the barge on the left.

The *Whitby Abbey* in dock with the warehouses and the church spire dominating the scene. A glimpse of the town can be seen to the left of the photograph.

The *Byland Abbey*, another of the group which frequented Goole Docks which were responsible for much of Goole's trade.

The SS *Dearne* is waiting to enter the docks when the tide reaches a suitable level.

The guide light was situated on a promontory near the end of the Dutch River and Ocean Lock. The ship to the right is heading away from Goole towards the River Humber and ultimately, the open sea.

The river and docks around the turn of the twentieth century. The 'Pepperpot Hoist' is prominent on the skyline to the left. People on The Promenade watch as a sailing ship is towed on the tide towards the River Humber and the North Sea.

The captain on his bridge surveys the scene as SS Yokefleet leaves port with its cargo. The panorama in its wake is interesting; it passes the mouth of the Dutch River at the end of Ocean Lock, a fine view of a 'Pepperpot Hoist' and a number of barges to add to the activity.

Four

Hook

Hook is situated on a strip of land formed by a loop in the River Ouse as it approaches Goole.
In 1213 the Abbot of Selby allowed Baron John de Houke of the manor to build a chantry
chapel. The de Houke family were of Norman origin and it is from them that the village takes
its name. It is said that a monastery once stood in a field by the church which had a moat.
This view shows the High Street around 1900, with a farm building to the right and a village
shop displaying its wares to the left. Each cottage in the row had a long back garden in which
vegetables could be grown, a pig reared and chickens kept to augment the family income.
Beekeeping was also popular. Today very little of the old High Street remains.

HOOK.BRIDGE.

A committee, led by Alderman Moss of Hull, proposed in 1860 that a line should be built from Staddlethorpe on the Hull-Selby railway to Goole, providing Hull with a direct line to Doncaster and a connection to London. The scheme met with difficulties when the North Eastern Railway, fearing competition, offered an alternative plan in the form of the Lancashire Yorkshire Railway. The original plan was eventually realised and the Hull to Doncaster line, cutting around 20 miles off the journey to London, was opened on 30 July 1869. The Hull merchants were delighted. One of the chief difficulties during the line's construction was the erection of a swing bridge over the River Ouse from Skelton to Hook. The completed structure was, at one time, regarded as the 'largest double line railway bridge with moveable spans in the world' a slight exaggeration as there was at least one larger bridge. Built by Sir William Armstrong & Co. of Newcastle, Hook Bridge lies 2 miles north east of Goole. It had 5 fixed spans and a moveable portion of 2 spans. The fixed spans were of wrought iron plate supported by cast iron columns filled with cement; the moveable spans were built on a huge central pillar made up of 7 cast iron columns which was swung round on a 30 ft hydraulic turntable. It took about 1 min to open the channel to allow river traffic through. This portion was 250 ft long with a signal box at both the Skelton and Hook ends of the 830 ft bridge but, in 1933 a panel was installed in the central cabin and the boxes were closed. On 21 December 1973 tragedy struck in the form of a German coaster which collided with one of the fixed spans, which dropped onto the river bed, closing the bridge to river traffic until August 1974. British Rail were able to recover only 4 per cent of the repair and dislocation costs so, to general consternation, threatened to close the line between Gilberdyke and Goole in 1983. The issue was resolved in 1984 when Humberside County Council negotiated a financial settlement. Essential repairs took place but as these were nearing completion, on 23 November 1988, a ship became locked under one of the spans causing further damage and it was not until 2 October 1989 that normal traffic was resumed.

The bridge across Hook Road that carried the railway line between Hull and Goole was a much easier engineering proposition than the river bridge. Although just as necessary as the Ouse Bridge, it presented none of the problems caused by the river.

A note on the back of this postcard tells us that it shows Hook Feast, 1925. There was a playing field beside the church which was always the scene of activity at the time of the feast. Over the years this activity varied, featuring sports and musical entertainments, including a hurdy gurdy: all aimed at every member of the family, young and old.

St Mary's church, Hook, has some thirteenth century features and examples of the Early English and Perpendicular styles, but was heavily restored in the nineteenth century. It is pleasantly situated facing the River Ouse on the road leading to Boothferry Bridge.

Funeral cortege in Hook churchyard. Judging by the number of spectators present, the deceased was well known and respected.

This sad little plot in St Mary's churchyard, Hook, marks the graves of cholera victims who died in the epidemic of 1932. Each of the small, square, sandstone stones is marked with a large Roman letter 'C'. It is said that the graves were not to be disturbed for at least 100 years. The disease was carried from Asia to the Baltic and, in 1831, is thought to have been carried to Britain by some unfortunate traveller, perhaps a seaman. Cholera had a reputation for spreading at a frightening rate and cases were soon being reported all over the country. By February 1832 it had reached London, leaving a trail of victims in its wake. As similar gravestones across the country testify, many villages like Hook were ravaged by the disease which, once contracted, caused high fever, cramps and spasms in the limbs, violent diarrhoea, vomiting, thickening of the blood and death soon after.

It was not until 1893 that a vaccine to prevent cholera was developed by the German bacteriologist Robert Koch (1843–1910). The germ causing the disease it was decided could be carried by dirty water, tainted food and by infection in families. Prior to the discovery of the vaccine fresh air was recommended as being the only way to avoid the disease. Since the nineteenth century Britain has escaped its scourge.

Five

Howden and Selby

Composite view of Howden during the early part of this century, showing the main features of the town and the ferry.

There was a church at Howden as early as the eighth century. When William the Conquerer invaded Britain, Howden was just a few dwellings in a marshy area. In 1080 he gave the church to the Bishop of Durham, one Walter Skirlaw who is reputed to have been the son of a basket maker from the East Yorkshire village of Skirlaugh. The bishop, who was interested in buildings, planned and paid for much of the church but died whilst the workmen were still raising the central tower. The Priory and Convent of Durham were responsible for setting up a collegiate foundation for priests and the church became a minster. The edifice, dedicated to St Peter, has suffered in many ways. In 1696 part of the roof of the old choir collapsed and further damage was caused by Oliver Cromwell's troops billeted there during the Civil War. In 1750 the spire and roof of the Chapter House fell down and the minster narrowly escaped complete destruction in 1929 when an arsonist started a fire there, allegedly because of some imagined slight he had suffered in the town. This view shows the minster early this century before the arson attack.

Right: Doorway to the Chapter House of Howden Minster which suffered the ravages of neglect when the spire and part of the roof collapsed in 1750.

Below: Howden was, for a long time, famous for its Great Horse Fair where the trading of Yorkshire horses continued well into the nineteenth century. During this time the town had numerous inns such as the Bowman's Hotel, seen here, which changed its name from the Nags Head; its yard once provided stabling for eighty-five horses and contained a blacksmiths. John Bowman also hired out gigs and carriages which met every train after the railway station was opened in 1840 and the hotel was a Royal Mail Posting House. Next door is the Wellington, formerly the White Hart; its name was changed in 1823 to commemorate the Battle of Waterloo. It too had stables and was a coaching inn when the stagecoach Eclipse carried passengers to Hull and Liverpool.

An 1868 advertisement from the Howden printer C.S. Sutton of Market Place, who was obviously well patronised by both gentry and the general public. In his list of services he includes pictures frames and cartes de visites, an early form of photographic visiting card popular at the end of the nineteenth century. He was also the office of the *Howdenshire Gazette* and the agent for other newspapers including the *Yorkshire Post*.

Howden is a place of antiquity. In 959 AD, King Edward of Mercia granted land in 'Hoveden' to a lady known locally as Quen. King John later gave Bishop de Peitou of Durham, Lord Howden, the right to hold a fair and a market in the town and it is thought that John Wesley preached from the Market Cross when he visited the town in 1776.

Parsons Lane, Howden, around the turn of the twentieth century, was a pleasant walkway from the church to nearby farms and houses.

This poignant image shows the nose of the airship R38 leaving its shed at Howden at about 7.00 am on the day of the ill fated flight which ended tragically at 5.35 pm on Wednesday 24 August 1921 over the River Humber. Built at Cardington, it was the largest rigid airship constructed at that time and was based at Howden whilst undergoing trials before being handed over to the US Navy as the ZR2. It measured 695 ft in length with a capacity of 2,700,000 cu ft of gas. As it passed over the pier at Hull, at a height of 600 ft, a terrific explosion occurred; some eyewitnesses stated that it cracked open like an egg and then fell in flames into the river. Of the forty-nine British and American personnel on board, there were only five survivors.

Above: Mr George Parkin of Brenda House, Howden, tending his sheep. The area immediately surrounding the market town was predominantly agricultural; in recent years there has been a move towards horticulture and market gardening.

Right: The symbolic sighting of the three swans (see next page) by Benedict is reflected by the coat of arms of Selby Abbey which is described thus: Sable (black) three swans close argent (silver).

**ARMS OF
SELBY ABBEY**

sable three swans close argent

Selby Abbey.

Selby Abbey, the church of St Mary and St Germaine, seen from the pleasant park which runs alongside and leads down to the railway station. A Benedictine abbey was established on the site around 1070 by Benedict of Auxerre. The present building was started in 1100 and also combines fine work from the fourteenth century; the upper part of the tower was rebuilt after it collapsed in 1690. The story goes that when Benedict sailed up the River Ouse, he saw three swans in the air who suddenly landed. Taking this as a sign he planted a cross and built his hut there. William of Normandy, who owned the land, made him abbot and donated the land on which to build his church. The town of Selby then developed around the abbey and on Mondays the weekly market took place around the cross in front of the abbey's edifice. The prosperity of the area derives from the surrounding agricultural land, its flour and animal feed mills and later, coal.

Monday is traditionally market day in Selby. The Market Cross, erected in 1790 by the Lord of Londsborough, Robert Edward Petrie, replaced the cross erected at the granting of the Market Charter by Edward II in 1324; as in many market towns, it has become a meeting place for the town's people over the years. The magnificent abbey dominates the scene but the imposing building on the left belongs to Barclays Bank. The town originally developed around the abbey and much of its prosperity was linked with the shipping to and from Goole along the River Ouse.

A later view, around the 1950s. The scene is similar but the atmosphere has changed. There are now parked cars and a lorry approaches on the right. The buildings, including the Londsborough Arms near the abbey, appear smarter.

Above: This misericord carving in the church of the Blessed Virgin Mary at Hemingborough is thought to be the oldest example of such woodcarving in the country. The symmetrical design of conventional foliage dates from the thirteenth century and in style is reminiscent of the earlier Romanesque or late Norman decoration. Ths wonderful carving is not the church's only claim to fame; the fourteenth century 60 ft tower supports a 190 ft spire, which has become a landmark in this very flat area. The village is thought to have derived its name from Walter de Hemingborough, an early chronicler.

Left: Stillingfleet, near Selby, stands on a little beck which flows into the River Ouse. The church of St Helen has, in the south porch, a unique door made from oak planks decorated with ornamental ironwork. Apart from the large hinges there is a floral knot and Viking longship containing two figures, the steering oar quite clearly defined. This door is thought to date back to the twelfth century and shows that earlier visits by the Vikings were still remembered in the area.

Six

Villages to the South

GOOLE RD, REEDNESS.

Reedness is next to Whitgift, and the charm of the village is apparent from this 1920s view of Goole Road. The really striking feature is the complete absence of traffic of any description, leaving the lone pedestrian in the foreground to his perambulations without fear of accident.

Epworth Rectory, c. 1900. Epworth village is south of Goole on the Isle of Axholme, which is linked to the town by an area of land drained by Vermuyden in the seventeenth century. John Wesley was born at the Old Rectory so it could be said that Methodism was born here. His father, Samuel, had a small living in South Ormsby, Lincolnshire, but offended a local nobleman by refusing to receive his mistress and moved to Epworth, where he lived and preached for many years. John was born on 17 June 1703; even as a child, he was a pious boy with an inquisitive mind who, at an early age, was well acquainted with the Bible. He served as his father's curate for a while but after missionary work in 1738, he began his task of converting Britain. He travelled extensively but spent a considerable amount of time and made many friends in the villages around Goole, using the Whitgift Ferry to cross the River Ouse. He once preached in Epworth using his father's tomb for his platform.

A 1920s view of the Wesley Memorial Church, Epworth, built in honour of the great preacher.

The last stones in England

First & Last House in England

John Wesley

THE LAND'S END
CORNWALL.
Where Wesley
wrote the well
known Hymn
"Lo! ON A
NARROW NECK
OF LAND."

A Memento
of
The Sojournings of
THE LATE
"JOHN
WESLEY"
In Cornwall.

Born on JUNE 17th 1703
Died in his 88th Year
MARCH 2nd 1791.

Lands End Point

This card endorses stories of John Wesley's travels, which covered the length and breadth of the country.

Whitgift is a quaint, old fashioned village which merges into equally picturesque Reedness. It stands beside the River Ouse and ships pass as they leave Goole on their seabound journeys. It is said that sailors on deck could check the time with the clock on the church tower which bore a Latin inscription, which, translated reads: 'Peace on Earth'. The magnificent Hall, or Manor House, is one of the most impressive buildings in the village.

Swinefleet is on the banks of the River Ouse where it is broad and deep after it leaves Goole. The ships from the port pass as they head for the River Humber and finally out to sea. The river between Goole and Swinefleet forms a loop and the spire of Goole Church and the tall cranes on the docks can be clearly seen from the village. Kings Causeway is a pleasant, leafy road leading into the main village.

The High Street, Swinefleet, consisted of brick houses with pantile roofs. The banks of the river were quite high in an attempt to prevent flood waters reaching the houses when the high tides of March and Deptember caused parts of the River Ouse to flood.

Seven

Villages to the West

(Cowick Church.

Cowick is a small village between Rawcliffe and Snaith. The village has had a hall since Tudor times, but in more recent years it became the offices of a large manufacturing company. It was an impressive building which was said to have in the park, traces of a tower built by John of Gaunt. Sir John Dawney of Cowick, who became Viscount Downe in 1680, is recorded as having played a leading role in the Restoration in 1660. The church, with its unusual lantern tower and steeply pitched roof, is of a later date.

Rawcliffe stands on the River Aire. This 1920s view shows what is now the busy main road from Goole into the West Riding. The church is surrounded by the village green, which was the scene of what was known locally as Rawcliffe's Feast. At this popular, annual event there were all the usual attractions like the shamrocks, cocks 'an 'hens, chairoplanes, coconut shies and a plethora of side shows. The Feast was an excuse for great cleaning and baking marathons as the womenfolk anticipated visits from relatives and friends: 'We just thowt w'ed pop in as we're at Feast'.

The chapel, or Rawcliffe Bridge Mission, winter, c. 1910. Turn left round the green as you pass Rawcliffe and you find yourself in Rawcliffe Bridge, which, while really a part of Rawcliffe village, was also a close knit community in its own right. The mission was a popular meeting place. There was a paper mill at Rawcliffe Bridge which provided employment for some of the local men as an alternative to traditional agricultural work.

Carlton Towers was built around 1614. A priest hole there indicates that the original family were supporters of Roman Catholicism. In Victorian times the building had a narrow escape when Henry, ninth Duke of Beaumont and architect William Welby Pugin had neo-Gothic architectural designs for the house. Fortunately they quarrelled and it fell to John Francis Bentley, the architect of Westminster Cathedral, to restore the old house. Mona Beaumont inherited Carlton Towers after her marriage to a future Duke of Norfolk and their descendants still live in the house. There was once a toll bridge in the village and a coaching inn, the Oddfellows Arms, which had a blacksmiths shop.

Village High Street, Carlton, with the spire of the parish church of St Mary clearly visible. There was originally a fourteenth-century chantry chapel on the site which was renovated in 1688 and improved by the Victorians in 1862. The inn is the Oddfellows Arms.

Snaith was an area particularly prone to flooding before Vermuyden cut his channel, redirecting the course of the River Aire between Snaith and Rawcliffe. Once a market town, the village still retains some of the old street names such as Beast fair, where there were once almshouses dating from 1627. This Edwardian view shows Raper's and Whitaker's shops on the left. Raper's offers Royal Daylight lamp oil and has a poster in the widow about a Mrs Barker. Note the pristine white apron worn by the young girl.

Snaith, c. 1921. The village boasted a school very early in its history, established by Nicholas Waller in 1626, the time of the marsh drainage. It was in use until 1877 and was later used as a church meeting room.

Edwardian view of a celebration gathering at St Lawrence's Church, Snaith. The clerestoried church is 170 ft long, built of light grey stone and the walls adorned with pinnacles and battlements. A stained glass window depicts the martyred St Lawrence with a flaming grid-iron and his Roman tormentors.

The Wesleyan Chapel at Snaith still stands and is little changed from the time it was built in 1842. Like many similar buildings it has played a large part in the lives of generations and is still used by the members of the community.

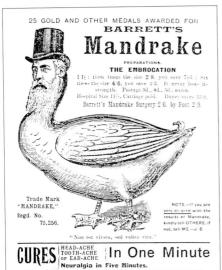

Left: The curious Man Drake bird, which was also a pun on the name of the folk medicine mandrake root, was the trademark of Snaith based Joshua Barrett FESS. It appears to have been a wonderful embrocation and universal cure-all for a wide variety of ailments including dyspepsia, rheumatism, biliousness, chronic liver diseases and ear ache.

Below: Thorne is another place which owes its existence in its present form to Vermuyden's marsh drainage scheme at Hatfield Chase. The Dutch River passes the town and the River Don is nearby. Thorne has a grammar school, founded in 1705, and is widely known for Thorne Colliery which, in its day, was reputed to be one of the four deepest coal mines in England, having a shaft of 3,000 ft. The church of St Nicholas which dominates the town, is Early English, with examples of work ranging from the twelfth, thirteenth and fifteenth centuries.

ST. NICHOLAS CHURCH, STONEGATE, THORNE

Eight

Villages to the North

ASSELBY. N.ª HOWDEN

Street in Asselby, near Howden; the house looks very new in this 1905 photograph. Everyone seems to be dressed in their Sunday best.

Bubwith is situated on the east bank of the River Derwent and its history can be traced back to Viking times. Barges plying between the ports of Goole, Hull and Malton passed through the village and rejoined the River Ouse at Barmby on the Marsh. Bulmer's Directory of 1892 records, 'There is a spacious wharf where boats discharge their cargoes of lime, gravel, coal etc.' There was a warehouse to the left of All Saints' Church which is twelfth century; the stone for its construction was brought up the river by barge.

Bubwith, showing the lay out of the village, which today is a thriving community. One of the traditions which still remains is the annual choice of the Village Queen on Gala Day.

Above: Considering the size and population of Bubwith, the school, seen here around 1920, was quite a spacious building. As with other schools of its type, the bell in the tower on the roof would be rung to hurry errant pupils to their classrooms.

Right: Before the tidal barrier was built at Barmby, some of the meadowland around Bubwith often flooded. This encouraged migrating birds, including some rare species, as well as rare grasses and wild flowers. Bubwith and the surrounding area was a farming community and one activity, which no longer exists, was the growing of teazels used for wool combing in the mills of the West Riding.

Wesleyan Chapel, Eastrington, 1903. John Wesley spent his last night at Eastrington with the family of his great friend Henry Bell of Partington Hall, which had a chapel that Wesley loved. Wesley was very fond of his friend's son, John Bell who at times rode with him, so it is hardly surprising to find a Wesleyan Chapel in the village.

Eastrington has always been agricultural and most men worked on the land until the end of the nineteenth century. Some villagers however, were employed making woollen cloth from the flax grown in the area. The village also had a mill and there are records of others working as carpenters, thatchers and brick and tile makers.

The church of St Michael, Eastrington, contains many interesting Norman, Saxon and medieval carvings. The first recorded vicar, Robert de Heyington, appears to have been appointed in 1318, although there was a church in the village as early as 1227.

The wooden building to the left is the parochial hall at Eastrington. The tall, central monument is the war memorial honouring those who died in the First World War; note the fresh flowers at its base. The church tower and churchyard belong to St Michael's Church.

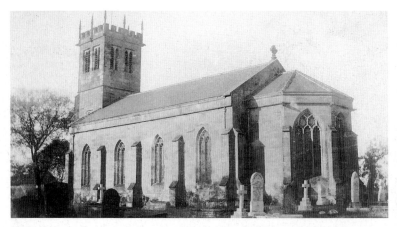

Blacktoft is a small place with a very long history. Around 1,200 years ago the Vikings set up a base there from which they could raid York. In the 1800s it became a small port in its own right, exporting flour to the Continent and importing Flemish tiles. The jetty was constructed in 1877 by the Aire and Calder Navigation to be used as a haven for ships en route to Goole in danger of being grounded by falling tides. This situation made smuggling very easy, giving rise to many stories and legends. St Clement's church was formerly called Holy Trinity; in 1237 William de Melsanby was installed as the first priest-in-charge. Disaster struck in 1839 in the form of a severe gale which brought down the top of the bell tower, destroying the roof. When the church was rebuilt, the windows and original arches were retained. It has three bells, the largest of which is dated 1500.

In spite of the ravages it has suffered over time, Wressle Castle is still an impressive building and is the only fortified castle still standing in the East Riding. From this view, which does not show too much of the devastation it has experienced, it is easy to accept that this fourteenth century structure has walls 6 ft thick; some of the transom windows are visible. Its construction is attributed to Thomas Percy, Admiral of the Fleet for Edward III.

Wressle Castle, now a sad ruin, was once the home of the influential Percy family, the Earls of Northumberland. It became uninhabitable at the end of the Civil War and was almost destroyed by fire in 1796.

The farmhouse which was built near the castle at a later date. There is a gentleman who appears to be a gardner, two ladies who are probably servants and, to the right, a lady enjoying the sun whilst working on a piece of embroidery. The farm was still being worked in the 1950s.

Tranquil view from the turn of the twentieth century of Barmby on the Marsh, a small village set where the River Derwent joins the River Ouse. Before drainage systems were installed, the surrounding marshlands, which are some of the richest in the area, would be flooded in winter and ice skating was enjoyed by young and old.

Postcard of the High Street, Barmby, 1910, sent by the lady who lived in the house marked with the cross and who signs herself, 'Minnie'. The gentleman with the handcart in the traffic free street has conveniently paused along his way outside the public house. Barmby seems to have been a lively place; during the summer, commencing on the last Thursday in June, there was horse racing. Like other villages, it had its Feast Day – a joyful occasion with a fun fair and an influx of visitors to add to the festivities.

The vicarage of St Helen's church, Barmby on the Marsh, in about 1909, with its very fine Monkey Puzzle tree. In the churchyard there are two wells: St Helen's Well, which gives water from a spring rich in iron and St Peter's Well, said to ensure health and long life to drinkers as a result of its high sulphur content. There is a firm belief that these wells protected the population of the village from an outbreak of cholera which ravaged the area in 1854.

KNEDLINGTON MANOR.

Knedlington is best described as a hamlet built on both sides of the Barmby Road. The impressive Knedlington Manor dates from the seventeenth century; this early twentieth-century view shows the interesting gables which give a rather Dutch appearance to the house.

Howden Dyke Ferry.

Holroyd & Ase
Real Photo Se

The ferry boat from Howdendyke in 1912 appears to have crossed the River Ouse in a diagonal course to Hook; there are signs of what was possibly a wharf and landing place on the bank there. Little is left on the Howdendyke side, although there is an old post down Ferry Lane. Today it is quite a busy place with a wharf where ships of up to 2,500 tons, mainly from Europe, discharge their cargoes.